HAPPINESS IS A *Horse*

HAPPINESS IS A
Horse

CHRISTIANE SLAWIK

🌿 **WILLOW CREEK PRESS**

Published by Willow Creek Press
P.O. Box 147, Minocqua, Wisconsin 54548

For information on other Willow Creek Press titles,
call 1-800-850-9453

Printed in Canada

Special thanks to

Silvia Hümmert, Christine Fischer, Barbara Stimpfel, Daniela Bolze,

Svea Lunburg, Maren Schulze, Regina Johannsen, Andrea Jänisch,

Marlit Hoffmann, Annette und Larissa Platen, Andrea Schmitz,

Ina Krueger-Oesert, Suzanne Struben, Bellinda Weymanns,

Susanne Schruefer, Marisol Lopez, Alfons Dietz, Eberhard Weiss,

Richard Hinrichs, Lisl Stabinger, Magda Strakova and many others

for sharing their personal happiness with me and other horse lovers!

Christiane Slawik

Happiness

Being able to find one's joy in someone else's joy is the secret of happiness. This is why there are so many happy horse lovers. If you keep, handle, and train horses according to their nature, and approach them with open eyes and ears as well as an open heart, they communicate very clearly that they feel happy. From the ten-year-old girl to the riding master, they all have something in common— the happiness they are given by these wonderful animals.

There is

nothing better
than getting your horse
out of the stable at the break of dawn,
hearing him snort contentedly,
and merging with him while
riding toward the sun together...

Their eyes
mirror my soul.

I am always

thrilled

at their quiet way of communicating.
Wiggling an ear says more
than a thousand words.

Horses are

fiery and gentle,

wild and docile at the same time.

With this unique nature of theirs,

they fill my heart with joy

every day anew.

The passion

for horses is a seed within you
that never dies, but buds over and over again,
no matter what life holds in store for you.

Horses live in their own world but nonetheless allow us to share it.

Horses are

especially faithful companions.

They don't argue, but listen.

They can also heal bruised souls.

A horse's back is the best medication for sadness.

Their joy
is contagious.

The most *wonderful* thing in the world for a rider is dreaming of a gallop along the seashore. And what is even better is when the dream comes true!

Sometimes, you don't believe in yourself,

and others don't believe in you.

It seems nobody listens to you, and

nobody loves you or trusts you.

But always, you believe in your horse,

and your horse believes in you.

Always, your horse listens to you.

Your horse loves you.

Your horse trusts you.

He gives you his unconditional

heart.

They have so much

power...

...and even more

character.

Horses bring me down to earth
and yet, at the same time,
make me
fly with joy.

Loving horses
is a fire burning inside you that always

keeps you warm and never dies.

Horses are
so thoroughly honest and without distrust,
such as no human is capable of being.

Watching horses in the field for one hour
is better than seeing a psychotherapist.

When I am with my horse,

I can forget everything

around me.

When it seems as if your soul has merged
with your horse's power while riding,
there is nothing but

infinity ahead.

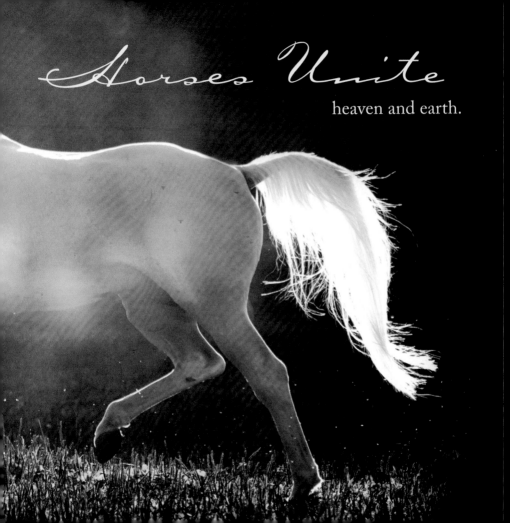

Horses Unite

heaven and earth.

Loving horses is

unconsciously following hoof prints while out for a walk,
and clicking your tongue to help your car go uphill.

It's difficult to conceive their wealth of

mysteries.

What a great feeling

to be allowed to sit on their backs

and let the wind caress my face.

Horses remind

me to live every moment in the here and now.

Horses grow

together with their rider—
and together they surpass themselves.

No other animal conveys such an amount of

positive energy,

or releases so many positive feelings.
They radiate a spirit of adventure,
joy of life, and movement.

In the evening,

I bring in the horses from the field.

Their coats smell of summer,

wind and fresh grass.

Horses always
succeed in spoiling my bad mood.

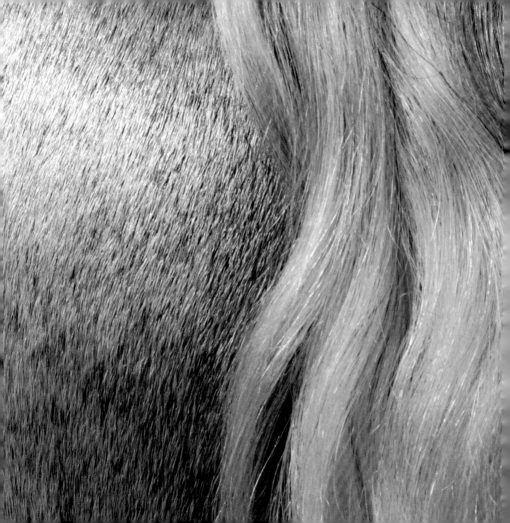

Their manes

are as long as I have always wished mine to be.

With horses,

you experience the seasons much more intensively.
The colder it is, the more spirited they become.
What a sight when their warm breath drifts
through the cold air like a white flag.

Horses

accompany you through

life without ever saying,

"I can't be bothered."

Life is too short
to make do without such
wonderful beings as horses.

Our wealth

does not jingle—

but welcomes us with a nicker every day.

There are many
people who steal my energy—
Horses give it back to me.

Working with horses is like meditation.
In their sereneness and power
I also discover my own

strength.

If only we let them, they will turn us into better *human beings.*

Their beauty

Horseback riding is the perfect fusion between

nature and art.

Every second you spend with a horse

is appreciated.

They satisfy

their wonderful curiosity like little children,

experiencing life through all their senses.

Horses give us physical and spiritual *warmth.*

Horses send me
to cloud nine.

No matter how much money you have or in what phase
of life you are in, you will always find a horse who
matches you.

The end

of a wonderful day:

cantering together towards sunset.